FRIENDLY FOES

A LOOK AT POLITICAL PARTIES

By Elaine Landau

L LERNER PUBLICATIONS COMPANY • MINNEAPOLIS

For Sarah Sutin

Lerner Publications Company
A division of Lerner Publishing Group
241 First Avenue North
Minneapolis, MN 55401 U.S.A.

Website address: www.lernerbooks.com

Library of Congress Cataloging-in-Publication Data

Landau, Elaine.
    Friendly foes : a look at political parties / By Elaine Landau.
       p.   cm. — (How government works)
       Summary: Describes the history and platforms of the two major political parties in the United States (Democrats and Republicans) as well as the bigger third-party movements.
       Includes bibliographical references and index.
       ISBN: 0-8225-1349-8 (lib. bdg. : alk. paper)
       1. Political parties—United States—Juvenile literature. 2. Democratic Party (U.S.)—Juvenile literature. 3. Republican Party (U.S.: 1854–)—Juvenile literature. [1. Political parties. 2. Democratic Party (U.S.) 3. Republican Party (U.S.: 1854)] I. Title. II. Series.
    JK2261 .L348 2004
    324.273—dc21   2002151706

Manufactured in the United States of America
1 2 3 4 5 6 – DP – 09 08 07 06 05 04

TABLE OF CONTENTS

INTRODUCTION

Picture a room filled with people. It is decorated with red, white, and blue streamers. Waiters bring out food on trays. A large cake is in the corner. It is shaped like an American flag.

There is a band at the front of the room. The musicians play "Yankee Doodle Dandy." People sing and sway to the music. They hug one another. Some wave small American flags. They are laughing and smiling.

(*Above*) Political parties rely on many people to support their members and make campaigns successful.

One man is the center of attention. He speaks to everyone there. He shakes their hands, too. This man is running for political office. He wants the support of these people. He needs their help to win the election.

These people are at a special party. This party has been given by an organized group of people known as a political party. That's right. It's a party given by a party. It may sound strange. But political parties give lots of parties.

Political parties do more than that, however. They play an important role in the United States. Political parties help determine who our elected officials will be. They also help determine how the nation is governed. This is a book about political parties—their past, present, and future.

New York senator Charles E. Schumer shakes a supporter's hand. Schumer is a Democrat. Almost all politicians are members of a political party.

CHAPTER 1
POLITICAL PARTIES

QUICK QUESTION: Have you ever thought about how the country should be run? Some people think the government should do a lot. They might want the government to provide health care to all citizens, for example. That way no one would have to worry about paying costly hospital bills. Some people might also want better government control of businesses.

That would mean stricter rules to protect consumers (customers). Higher wages and shorter hours for workers might be another of this group's goals.

(*Above*) Debates, such as this one in Louisiana, are one way political parties offer voters a chance to learn about candidates.

Others feel quite differently. They think people and businesses do best on their own. For them, less government is better government. They don't want the government involved in their everyday affairs. They also don't want the government too involved in businesses. They call that "big government." They believe that big government is bad government. Still other people want something in between.

LIFE IN A DEMOCRACY

The government of the United States is a democracy. In a democracy, the people rule. There are no kings and queens here. Instead, the people choose—or elect—those who will govern them. But everyone cannot be expected to agree on things. People's ideas about the government's

By voting for political candidates, every U.S. citizen can participate in our democratic government.

role will always differ. So will opinions on issues affecting the nation.

Individuals need a way to make their voices heard. Citizens want to elect officials who truly represent them. They want a government that reflects their ideas and opinions. They want the government to run the country the way they feel is best. People accomplish this through political parties. Parties are formed by people who share similar views. Individuals in a party work toward a common goal. The goal is to gain control of the government.

GIVING VOTERS A CHOICE

In a democracy like the United States, voters choose the political party they want to support. Each party chooses

Election ballots show voters their choices of candidates from different political parties.

candidates to run for office against candidates chosen by the other parties. Each candidate represents his or her party's ideals. Candidates run for different offices at all levels of government. Some candidates run for mayor in small towns. Others run for governor of a state. Still others run for president of the United States.

Major political parties nominate (choose) presidential candidates every four years. The parties do this at their national con-

Richard Nixon *(left)* and Spiro Agnew *(right)* were chosen as the Republican presidential and vice presidential candidates at the 1968 Republican National Convention.

ventions. National conventions are important political events, where party members gather. Delegates, or party representatives, come from every state and U.S. territory to choose candidates for president and vice president.

Did You KNOW? Some countries have just one political party. That's how it is in China. The party chooses the nation's leaders. The people cannot openly disagree with the government. If they do, they can be sent to prison.

Delegates also put together the party platform. Don't let that word confuse you. It's not a real wooden platform for candidates to stand on. Instead, it's a list of ideas that the

IN A DEMOCRACY . . .

The political party that has the most members in Congress is called the majority party. The party with fewer members in Congress is called the minority party. The minority party looks ahead to the next election. It also carefully watches the majority party. The minority party points out the other party's mistakes. It stresses how it would do things differently. Well-known minority party members regularly speak up. Their comments appear in newspapers. They also do television interviews. At the same time, the majority party uses the media to defend its position. This give-and-take is important in a democracy. It keeps the party in power on its toes. It also reminds voters that there are other choices at the next election. This makes for good government.

party stands for. It states the party's goals and values. Party platforms help voters understand what each party thinks about the issues.

HELPING WITH CAMPAIGNS

Well before election day arrives, party members plan and organize. They form small groups called campaign committees. These committees do many different jobs. One important job is raising money for the candidates. Political campaigns cost lots of money. Candidates need flyers to let voters learn their views.

Democratic senator Tom Daschle was the senate minority leader in 2003.

Sometimes candidates create ads that say negative things about their opponents. This TV ad for Senate candidate Rick Lazio of New York accuses his opponent, Hillary Rodham Clinton, of creating a negative campaign.

Candidates also pay for ads in magazines and newspapers. They buy radio and television time to run their ads. They may also have websites on the Internet.

All these measures are important, however. Many voters never meet the people they vote for. The media is often the only way for voters to learn about candidates. So parties do their best to raise money for publicity.

Did You KNOW? Major political parties in the United States spend big bucks on campaigns. Some campaigns have cost millions of dollars!

Yet, whenever possible, political parties do want voters to meet their candidates. Another job of campaign committees is to arrange rallies and tours for candidates to speak to people directly.

At these events, candidates give speeches to try to win people's votes.

All political parties dream of victory on election day. At victory parties, people smile and congratulate one another. But even if its candidate wins, the party's work still isn't done. Not even after the confetti is cleaned up and the last folding chair is put away. There is still a lot to do.

SUPPORTING THEIR CANDIDATES

After elections political parties support their elected officials and the laws they want to get passed. The party defends its officeholders when other parties

Find out about political parties in your state. Visit <http://www.politics1.com/parties.htm>

DIG DEEPER

criticize them. The party also provides its elected representatives with expert political advice. Political parties don't just want their candidates to be elected. They want them to succeed in office and be reelected in the future. By doing this, political parties can keep and build on their power and influence.

CHAPTER 2
THE BEGINNING
OF POLITICAL PARTIES

TRUE OR FALSE? The United States has always had at least two political parties, right? False. There were no political parties here when our nation was born. The Founding Fathers distrusted them. The Founders viewed political parties as special interest groups not concerned with the common good.

These early leaders wanted a strong, united country. They believed political parties would divide the nation. They wanted people to do what was best for

At the time of the signing of the Declaration of Independence *(above)*, the Founding Fathers did not believe in political parties.

the entire nation rather than what might be good for a particular political party.

That was the Founders' dream. But that's not exactly what really happened. Building a new nation was not easy. People often saw things differently. Those with similar views naturally joined together. They knew there was power in numbers. Before long they began to form—you guessed it—political parties.

PEOPLE FILE George Washington, our first president, disliked political parties. He never joined one. Just before leaving office, he warned that political parties would destroy the nation.

THE FEDERALIST PARTY

The Federalist Party, led by Alexander Hamilton, was probably the nation's first political party. The Federalists were concerned about national security (the safety of our country) and unity among the states. They wanted a strong federal, or national, government. They also favored business people rather than farmers.

Alexander Hamilton was the leader of the Federalist Party. He wrote a series of essays on Federalism called the *Federalist Papers*. Later on, he also became our country's first secretary of the treasury.

The Federalists did not trust ordinary people. They felt the government should be run by the rich, well-educated upper class. This was an elite group of Americans. The Federalists believed they would make the wisest decisions. They only wanted to see people like themselves in public office. The Federalists controlled the new government from 1789 to 1801.

THE DEMOCRATIC-REPUBLICAN PARTY

Some Americans, including Thomas Jefferson and James Madison, disagreed with the Federalists. They wanted to form a new party. It became known as the Democratic-Republican Party. The word *republican* remained in the party's name until the 1820s. Then the party split into several groups. But many people think that the Democratic-Republican Party was actually the start of the modern Democratic Party. (Others disagree.)

"SOUND BYTE" Thomas Jefferson was against political parties. In 1789 he said, "If I could not go to heaven but with a party, I would not go there at all."

The Democratic-Republicans were not like the Federalists. They were ordinary folks. Most were workers, small farm owners, or craftsmen.

The Democratic-Republicans did not want a strong federal government. They believed that the views and voices of all the people should count. The Federalists did not represent these people. The Democratic-Republicans wanted a government that represented all Americans—not just the wealthy.

Thomas Jefferson

Thomas Jefferson had helped form the new party. Jefferson was not like most of the Democratic-Republicans. He was not an average worker. Jefferson was well-off and owned a large plantation. But Jefferson believed that ordinary people could govern themselves. He wanted a political party that was the "party of the common man."

THE FEDERALISTS FIGHT BACK

The Democratic-Republicans opposed many Federalist Party ideas. The Federalists reacted. They had hoped to stay in power and did not want another political party to form. In 1798 the Federalists passed laws to try to break up the new party. These laws were known as the Alien and Sedition Acts.

Both of these acts made it illegal to publically criticize the Federalist Party. Anyone who did so could be jailed. Members of the new party paid a price for speaking out.

Did You KNOW? When our country was founded, women were not allowed to take part in politics. They were not allowed to be members of political parties, and they were not allowed to vote. Things have certainly changed!

Several newspaper editors were put in prison. These men had dared to criticize the Federalists in their writings.

THE DEMOCRATIC-REPUBLICANS GAIN POWER

Many people were outraged. The colonists wanted freedom. That included free speech. Many people did not want the Federalists to take charge. They wanted new leaders. And they got them. In 1800 Thomas Jefferson was elected president. Jefferson quickly freed all the jailed newspaper editors. The Federalists had failed. They could not make the United States a nation with just one party.

The people liked Jefferson. He was elected to serve a second term. Then in the 1808 presidential election, another Democratic-Republican, James Madison, won. He had been secretary of state under Jefferson.

In the Democratic-Republicans, ordinary people felt they had a party of their own. Because there were more working people in the United States than wealthy ones, the Democratic-Republican Party thrived. The Federalists continued to lose support. Over time their party became less and less important.

But by the late 1820s, trouble began to brew among the Democratic-Republicans. This time it had nothing to do with the Federalists. There were problems with the party itself. Various factions, or groups, within the Democratic-Republicans had begun quarreling. Each group wanted a different person to be the party's presidential candidate.

ANDREW JACKSON

One faction supported a man named Andrew Jackson. Jackson was elected president in 1828 and 1832. By then Jackson and his party were just called Democrats. The name stuck.

JACKSON TICKET

Honor and gratitude to the man who has filled the measure of his country's glory—*Jefferson*

FOR THE ASSEMBLY
GEORGE H. STEUART,
JOHN V. L. McMAHON.

Andrew Jackson had been a military hero during the War of 1812. The fame he gained in the war helped him win the presidency in 1828.

Jackson was truly a man of the people. All the earlier presidents had been wealthy. But Jackson was the son of poor Scotch-Irish immigrants. Jackson's followers included small farmers and large plantation owners, city laborers, and bankers. They shared many beliefs. But many Democrats disagreed with each other about slavery, banking rules, and tariff rates. (Tariffs are taxes on imports, or goods entering the United States from other countries.)

Jackson organized the Democrats into a strong national organization—the Democratic Party. Voters elected Democrats to be president several times in the 1800s—Martin Van Buren in 1836, James K. Polk in 1844, Franklin Pierce in 1852, and James Buchanan in 1856. The Democratic Party also held the majority of seats in Congress during much of that time.

An Inauguration to Remember

Andrew Jackson liked being among the people. He was elected president for the first time in 1828. In 1829 more than twenty thousand Americans turned out to see him take the oath of office. An inaugural party was held at the White House afterward. It was not like inaugural parties of the past, which powerful politicians and wealthy people had attended. This one was open to the public.

Thousands of people pushed their way into the White House. The crowd became unruly. Liquor spilled on the floor. Fights broke out, and china got smashed. Men in muddy boots stood on the fancy White House furniture. They just wanted to catch a glimpse of their new president.

Those closer to the president hoped to shake his hand. But Jackson had too many admirers. They pressed up against him. Several women fainted. But there didn't seem to be a way out. All the doors were blocked with people. So some people left through the windows.

Yet the Democrats saw the event as a great moment in history. One newspaper reported, "It was a proud day for the people. General Jackson is their own president."

Andrew Jackson's inaugural party at the White House

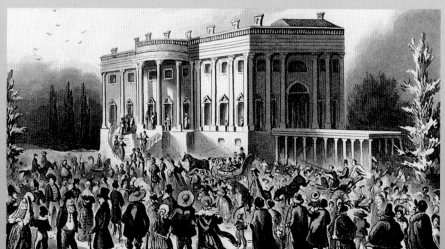

THE REPUBLICAN PARTY

Not everyone agreed with Andrew Jackson's politics. After he was elected president, several political groups that opposed him joined together. They formed their own political party—the Whig Party. The Whig Party lasted in the United States from about 1834 to 1856.

However, as time passed, the Whigs argued about slavery. To many Southern Americans, slavery was a part of their way of life. Families in the South earned most of their money from raising crops on large farms called plantations. Slaves did all the backbreaking work on these farms. Many Southerners saw slaves as property, not as workers. Some Southern Whigs were slaveholders. They left the Whig Party. Many of them joined the Democratic Party. Although the Democratic Party was also divided about slavery, it was popular in the South in the 1850s.

This cartoon shows the Whig Party as a cart. The men in the cart can't agree in which direction to go on the issue of slavery.

Many Northerners, including some Northern Whigs, were strongly against slavery. They formed a new party—the Republican Party—in the 1850s.

NEGROES
FOR SALE.

I will sell by Public Auction, on Tuesday of next Court, being the 29th of November, *Eight Valuable Family Servants*, consisting of one Negro Man, a first-rate field hand, one No. 1 Boy, 17 years o' age, a trusty house servant, one excellent Cook, one House-Maid, and one Seamstress. The balance are under 12 years of age. They are sold for no fault, but in consequence of my going to reside North. Also a quantity of Household and Kitchen Furniture, Stable Lot, &c. Terms accommodating, and made known on day of sale.

Jacob August.
P. J. TURNBULL, *Auctioneer.*
Warrenton, October 28, 1859.

Printed at the *News* office, Warrenton, North Carolina.

Slaves were sold, like property, at public auctions. As time passed, the question of whether to keep slavery legal or make it illegal became an important political issue for all parties.

In 1856 the Republicans ran their first candidate—John Frémont—for president. Frémont lost the election. However, he had gotten one-third of all the votes. This gave Republicans hope for future elections.

The issue of slavery divided Northern (antislavery) Democrats from Southern (proslavery) Democrats. In 1860 Northern Democrats nominated Stephen A. Douglas of Illinois for president. Southern Democrats nominated John C. Breckinridge of Kentucky. Republicans nominated a tall, bearded lawyer from Illinois. He was outspoken and firmly against slavery. His name was Abraham Lincoln. Lincoln was the first Republican to win the presidency.

"SOUND BYTE" In 1856 Republican presidential candidate John C. Frémont had a catchy antislavery campaign slogan. It was "Free soil, free labor, free speech, free men, Frémont."

ABRAHAM LINCOLN,

REPUBLICAN CANDIDATE FOR PRESIDENT OF THE UNITED STATES.

CHAPTER 3
THE REPUBLICAN PARTY

QUICK QUESTION: Is the Republican Party younger than the Democratic Party? Yes, but it took root quickly. It soon became just as important and powerful.

Abraham Lincoln's election as president was a major victory for the new Republican Party. But the country did not remain united under Lincoln. The month after he took office, the Civil War began. It lasted four years (1861–1865). On April 9, 1865, General Robert E. Lee of the South's

> Abraham Lincoln *(above)* was our country's first Republican president. At the time of his election in 1860, the Republican Party was quite new.

"**SOUND BYTE**" When Abraham Lincoln became president, slavery was allowed in fifteen states. It was banned in nineteen other states. Lincoln called the country "a house divided."

Confederate Army surrendered to General Ulysses S. Grant of the North's Union Army, and the Civil War came to an end.

PIONEERS AND BUSINESS OWNERS

In 1868 Grant was elected president. Black people gained the right to vote. Settlers headed west to develop new parts of the nation. The Republican Party became popular. It favored giving land to the settlers.

Large business owners from the North liked the Republican Party. Its policies helped them. In later years, the Republican Party would often be referred to as the party of "big business."

Republicans were elected president between 1877 and 1885. Republican presidents raised tariffs on imports (foreign goods). Because imports were costly, buyers chose cheaper American goods instead. This led to better sales of U.S. goods, and that made business owners happy with the high tariffs.

Business owners were attracted to the Republican

THE RAILROAD

One business—the railroad industry—profited greatly from Republican presidencies. The Republicans wanted a transcontinental railroad. This system would stretch from one side of the country to the other. In 1862 Congress passed the Pacific Railroad Act. This gave the job of building the railroad to two companies—the Union Pacific and the Central Pacific Railroads. Congress gave these companies huge sections of free land and lots of money in government loans. The railroad was completed on May 10, 1869.

Party for another reason, too. The party favored a strong banking system. This was important to keep businesses stable and on track.

REFORM

President Theodore (Teddy) Roosevelt became president in 1901. He had been vice president when Republican president William McKinley was shot and killed in September of that year. Roosevelt automatically became president. In 1904 he ran for the office of president and was elected.

Roosevelt was a Republican who supported laws to reform (change for the better) big business. Some businesses set high prices for their goods and services. They bought or crushed smaller companies that tried to compete with them. Soon only a few wealthy people controlled these big businesses, called monopolies. These businesses could charge as much as they wanted because they had no rivals. This practice hurt workers and farmers. Roosevelt was in favor of breaking up the monopolies. Roosevelt also supported laws to protect the environment and to protect people from impure food and drugs.

Teddy Roosevelt

Another Republican, William Howard Taft, was elected president in 1908. Republican candidates lost to the Democrats in 1912 and 1916. But Republicans won the presidency again after World War I (1914–1918).

DIG DEEPER In 1917 Republican Jeanette Rankin from Montana became the first woman to serve in Congress. That was three years before U.S. women got the right to vote.

THE ROARING TWENTIES

During the 1920s, the Republican Party won every presidential election and controlled Congress. Business was booming. The Republican Party helped big business by keeping taxes and government spending low. The Republicans also raised tariffs again. Many Americans seemed to be against trading with or helping foreign countries, against immigrants, and against workers' rights. The Republican Party represented those views.

Then in 1929, the stock market crashed, and the Great Depression began. People lost businesses, jobs, homes, farms, and their life savings. The Republicans lost power.

During the Great Depression, times were hard. Jobless people waited in line for free food *(left)*. Some had no money for new clothes *(below)*.

THE REPUBLICAN ORGANIZATION

The Republican Party is well organized. At the top is the Republican National Committee. It handles party business on a national level. Every state also has its own Republican State Committee. These committees have a chairperson and other workers. In addition, neighborhoods have Republican groups, which Republican precinct captains manage. On Election Day, the groups help get people out to vote. For example, they drive people to the polls if they need a ride.

GROWING STRONGER

The Republican Party was the minority party between 1933 and 1953, but it remained strong. During the 1950s, strong pockets of Republican voters grew in city suburbs. Suburbs are regions that developed around many of the nation's large cities after World War II (1939–1945).

Republican Dwight D. Eisenhower was a World War II hero. He won the presidency in 1952. Eisenhower even won the majority of votes in four Southern states, where Democrats usually won. He was reelected to a second term in 1956. Like other Republican presidents, Eisenhower encouraged business development. He also supported the first civil rights act since the period following the Civil War. This act set up the Commission on Civil Rights, which enforced civil rights laws (laws that make many kinds of discrimination illegal).

Richard M. Nixon was Eisenhower's vice president. In 1960 Nixon ran for president and lost. But he won in 1968 and again in 1972. Nixon favored spending money on the military and the space program. He reopened U.S. trade with China. But Nixon is probably best known for the Watergate scandal.

LEARN THE LINGO

The Republican Party is sometimes called the GOP. That stands for Grand Old Party. Republicans gave their party this nickname in the 1870s.

Watergate involved the break-in at the Democratic National Committee headquarters and the attempt to cover up the crime. Nixon resigned from office after it was found that he knew about the crime and the cover-up. Nixon's vice president, Spiro T. Agnew, had resigned earlier. He had been accused of taking illegal payments while in office and cheating on his income tax. These scandals were big blows to the Republican Party. The Republicans lost the presidential race in 1976. But they made a spectacular comeback with the election of Ronald Reagan in 1980 and again in 1984. Following President Reagan, Republican George H. W. Bush won in 1988.

From 1952 to 1992, the Republican Party did extremely well at the polls. For twenty-eight of those forty years, Republicans held the presidency. In 2000 George W. Bush was elected president. The Republican Party hopes to send many more of its candidates to Congress and the White House in the future.

Republican George W. Bush speaks with voters while on the presidential campaign trail in 2000.

Jefferson   Washington   Jackson

OUR COUNTRY'S CHOICE

GROVER CLEVELAND

THOMAS A. HENDRICKS

DEMOCRATIC NOMINEES

CHAPTER 4
THE DEMOCRATIC PARTY

TRUE OR FALSE? The Democratic Party changed as history unfolded. True—but it always remained the party of ordinary people. It probably reached its lowest point after the Civil War. As the war faded into history, however, the party gained strength. In contrast to the Republican Party, Democrats favored lower tariffs and laws to end dishonest business actions. In 1885 Grover Cleveland became the first Democratic president since 1856.

(Above) Campaign flyers, such as this one from 1884 for Democratic presidential candidate Grover Cleveland, were once drawn by hand.

During the 1900s and at the start of the 2000s, the Democratic Party became strongest in the nation's cities. Many immigrants, low-income workers, and minority groups live in cities. The Democratic Party has often fought for the rights of workers and poor people. This was especially true in the 1930s, during the Great Depression. The nation's economy was in a terrible state. Many banks closed, and businesses failed. People lost their homes and farms. Millions of people were out of work.

THE NEW DEAL

Democrat Franklin D. Roosevelt was elected president in 1932. During his time in office, he worked hard to improve the nation's economy.   Roosevelt started many programs— together called the New Deal—to put unem- ployed people back to work. Through these programs, the government created jobs for people who had none.   Some unemployed Americans built highways. Others

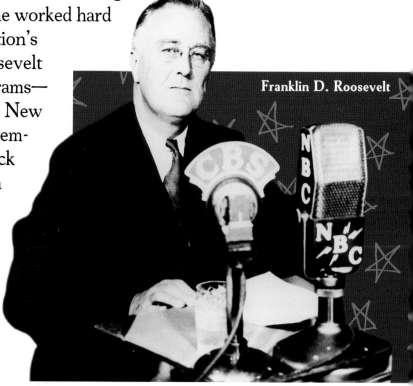

Franklin D. Roosevelt

Roosevelt's New Deal included a program called the Works Progress Administration (WPA). This agency put unemployed people to work doing public works. This WPA worker is planting trees.

built schools, bridges, dams, and parks. Artists, actors, writers, and musicians created new artworks.

During this time, the Democrats also passed improved labor laws. Workers were able to freely join labor unions (groups of workers organized to improve wages and working conditions). In the past, they had often been fired for doing so. Through unions, workers could fight for better pay and working conditions.

The Democrats passed the Social Security Act in 1935. This program served as a sort of safety net for Americans. Through Social Security, retired people received payments. Disabled people, children who had lost their parents, and others were helped, too.

THE FAIR DEAL

During World War II, Roosevelt concentrated on winning the war against Germany and Japan. When Roosevelt died on April 12, 1945, Vice President Harry S. Truman became president. Truman continued Roosevelt's policies, but he called his program the Fair Deal. Truman also fought for civil rights for black Americans. He won the 1948 election over Republican Thomas E. Dewey.

THE NEW FRONTIER

Democrat John F. Kennedy defeated Republican Richard M. Nixon in the 1960 presidential election. Kennedy introduced a reform program that he called the New Frontier. The program included helping poor areas of the country, increasing in the minimum hourly wage (the least amount of money employers can pay a worker), and reducing tariffs.

Kennedy also began the Alliance for Progress, a program to help countries in Central and South America build housing, power plants, and roads and to improve education and income. Despite supporting tax breaks for companies, Kennedy was thought to be antibusiness. On November 22, 1963, an assassin killed John Kennedy, and Vice President Lyndon B. Johnson was sworn in as president.

Democratic president John F. Kennedy started the Peace Corps. Through this program, Americans volunteer to go to poor countries in different parts of the world. They help people improve their communities. Here, Kennedy addresses a group of Peace Corps volunteers.

THE GREAT SOCIETY

Johnson developed a program called the Great Society to help poor and disadvantaged people. Among other things, it provided health care for senior citizens and the needy. Johnson also persuaded Congress to pass the Civil Rights Bill of 1964. It guaranteed equal rights for all Americans no matter what their race, religion, or gender.

Democratic president Lyndon Johnson signs the Civil Rights Bill of 1964.

THE PARTY PLATFORM

Helping ordinary people has long been part of Democratic Party platforms. Recent platforms have stressed job opportunities for workers, education improvements, and environmental protections. The platforms have also asked for low-cost child care and universal health care. That means that every man, woman, and child should have health insurance.

In 1968 Johnson chose not to run for reelection. Democratic candidate Hubert H. Humphrey lost the presidential election to Republican Richard M. Nixon.

The Democrats regained the White House in 1977 after Jimmy Carter, a peanut farmer from Georgia, defeated Republican Gerald R. Ford. But in 1980, the Democrats lost the presidency to Republican Ronald Reagan. Republicans held the presidency for twelve years until 1993. Then Bill Clinton won the presidency from Republican George H. W. Bush.

EIGHT GREAT YEARS

During President Bill Clinton's two terms in office (1993–2001), the U.S. economy was stronger than ever before. More people owned homes than in the past, and the number of crimes dropped. The Clinton administration created the most jobs ever under a single president. Americans also saw the largest drop in poverty in thirty years.

Did You KNOW? The Democratic Party has played a valuable role in America's history. It has had its share of important victories. Between the years 1800 and 2000, the Democrats won twenty presidential elections. The party is still going strong.

CHAPTER 5
REPUBLICANS AND DEMOCRATS: THE DIFFERENCES

TRUE OR FALSE? Republican programs favor different parts of the American population than Democratic programs do. True. Republican programs, such as high tariffs, often support big business owners. Democratic programs, such as raising the minimum hourly wage, usually support the workers. But the two major parties differ on many other issues, too.

Democrats and Republicans show their differences of opinion most strongly at political debates. *(Above)* Republican George H. W. Bush *(left)* argues with Democrat Michael Dukakis *(right)* in a televised presidential debate in 1988.

THE ROLE OF GOVERNMENT

The Republican Party favors "small" government. It believes

"that the best government is that which governs least." According to Republican beliefs, government should only provide people with services they cannot provide for themselves. What does small government mean in everyday life?

Republicans believe that too many government rules hurt businesses. Republicans want business to be free to operate without the government interfering. They feel thriving businesses mean more jobs. Republicans argue that everyone does better under those conditions.

Republicans also favor reducing government in other ways. They want the federal government to do less for people. Republicans want to return power and responsibility to the states. That means more decisions are made—and paid for—on a local level (by states and cities).

LIBERALS AND CONSERVATIVES

Democrats tend to be more liberal than Republicans. Liberals generally believe that the government needs to make rules for businesses to follow. They also want government programs to help people who are poor or sick. Republicans tend to be more conservative than Democrats. Conservatives generally believe that government should not interfere with businesses or with people's problems. They also want a strong military.

Former presidential candidate Pat Buchanan is a conservative.

The Democrats think differently. They believe some government rules are needed to protect workers and the environment. They stress that part of the role of government is to improve the lives of all its citizens. Democrats point to all the good that government programs have done. They argue that some programs help feed the hungry and house the homeless. Democrats feel that Americans are better off because of government programs.

GUN CONTROL

On some issues, such as gun control, the differences between Republicans and Democrats are clear. Most Republicans argue that Americans have the right to own guns. This right, they say, is guaranteed by the Second Amendment to the Constitution. They do not believe government

Democrats and Republicans disagree about whether people should be allowed to carry concealed (hidden) handguns.

should try to limit this right. They say this country already has enough gun control laws. No more government control is needed.

The Second Amendment says, "A well-regulated militia [military force], being necessary to the security of a free state, the right of the people to keep and bear arms shall not be infringed [limited]." Does this mean everyone should be able to own a gun? Or is the amendment talking about a militia using guns to defend the country? What do you think?

Most Democrats want stricter gun laws. The Democrats want to make it harder to buy guns. They want better background checks of gun buyers. They want to be sure that the buyer does not have a criminal record. They also want to be sure that the buyer does not have serious mental problems.

The Democrats also want to limit the types of guns that buyers can purchase. They stress that a duck hunter does not need a semiautomatic weapon. That type of gun was not designed for recreation. It was designed to kill people. They think such weapons should be controlled by strict gun laws.

TAXES

Running a country is expensive. People living in a nation pay for the services that their government provides. This is done through taxes. One important program that taxes pay for is Social Security. Another is Medicare. Medicare is a government-run health care program. It covers most people over sixty-five as well as some disabled people. Both parties agree that taxes are necessary. But they have different ideas about how much people should pay.

The Republicans favor keeping taxes low. They want Americans to pay as little for government programs as possible. They also want fewer programs. Republicans believe that Americans should keep more of their money. They think people will invest or spend it. This, they believe, will help the economy.

The Democrats take a different view. They believe properly spent taxes can help Americans. Taxes pay for important things, such as schools, courts, prisons, roads and bridges, parks, the space station, and the armed forces. Democrats also think that it is the government's duty to provide certain programs to help people. Republicans, in contrast, think people should take care of themselves. If they can't, then charitable groups can provide help.

Did You KNOW? The donkey is the Democratic Party's symbol. The elephant is the Republican Party's symbol. These symbols date back to the 1870s. A cartoonist named Thomas Nast used these animals to represent the parties. The cartoons appeared in a magazine called *Harper's Weekly.*

SPENDING

Political parties often argue about spending. The Republicans usually accuse the Democrats of spending too much money on too many programs. They call them the "tax and spend" party. The Republicans say that the Democrats will always raise taxes.

The Democrats say that the opposite is true. They argue that the Republicans spend a lot of money on their favorite issues, such as the military. Democrats stress that in recent years, Republican presidents have spent more than Democratic presidents. For example, Republican Ronald Reagan increased the budget deficit (created by the government spending more money than it takes in) to an all-time high of $200 billion in 1986. He cut government spending on welfare and unemployment programs. But he increased military spending.

The Democrats also note that in 2001 the government had extra money available. This is called a surplus. Democratic president Bill Clinton was in office from 1993 until 2001. Then Republican President George W. Bush took office. One year later, the surplus was gone. The deficit, or debt, quickly rose.

Republicans and Democrats will always disagree on some spending issues. But the parties also agree on some things. Both parties want a free and prosperous America. They just have different ideas about the best way to achieve that.

WHAT ARE YOU, ANYWAY?

Many people say they are Republicans or Democrats. They often vote for candidates from a particular party. They agree with that party's goals. They want that party to be in charge. Others actually become active in a party. They may volunteer their time. They often help with campaigns. These people send out mailings. They answer telephones. Some may even drive voters to the polls. They may contribute money to their favorite party or to a particular candidate within the party. They try to help their party succeed. Have you decided on a political party?

CHAPTER 6
THIRD PARTIES

QUICK QUESTION: What if you don't agree with the Republicans or the Democrats? You can still get involved. Smaller and less powerful parties—called third parties—would welcome you.

Third parties offer unique or controversial opinions. These parties often focus on one, specific issue. Sometimes the issue becomes important to the nation's two major parties as well.

(Above) The 2000 presidential election included third-party candidates on the ballot. Green Party nominees Ralph Nader and Winona LaDuke ran in this race.

Third parties have existed throughout much of our country's history. Often these parties were started for a specific purpose.

THE LIBERTY PARTY

The Liberty Party lasted only from 1840 to 1848. It was the earliest antislavery party. Its first national convention was held in Albany, New York, in 1840. The party platform dealt with just one issue—ending slavery.

The Liberty Party gained some strength over the years. James G. Birney was the party's presidential candidate in 1840 and 1844. He won sixty-two thousand votes in 1844. But the Liberty Party never became a threat to the two major parties. In 1848 the party met with other groups in Buffalo, New York. Together they formed another third party called the Free Soil Party.

James G. Birney

In some ways, the Free Soil Party picked up where the Liberty Party had left off. At the time, the country was still growing. New areas in the West were being settled. The Free Soil Party was against allowing slavery in these new territories. The party's slogan was "Free Soil, Free Speech, Free Labor, and Free Men." Many Free Soil supporters eventually joined the newly formed Republican Party.

THE SOCIALIST PARTY U.S.A.

Some third parties have been around for a long time. They often represent specific viewpoints. For example, the Socialist Party U.S.A. was organized in 1901. It was formed by members of the Social Democratic Party and the Socialist Labor Party. Socialists believe that workers and consumers should control production. They believe that the goods society produces should be used for the benefit of everyone, not for the private profit of a few people. The Socialist Party U.S.A. believes that "working people [must] organize for justice." Eugene V. Debs ran for president as a socialist candidate five times, in 1900, 1904, 1908, 1912, and 1920. He was never elected.

Eugene V. Debs, a member of the Socialist Party U.S.A., addresses a crowd of supporters in Milwaukee, Wisconsin, in 1925.

The Socialist Party U.S.A. introduced some ideas that were helpful to workers. Through the years, the party has fought against child labor, for better wages for workers, and for unemployment insurance. This insurance helps workers who have lost their jobs. The Democratic Party later adopted many of these ideas. As a result, American workers enjoy shorter hours and more benefits than in the past.

THE PROGRESSIVE PARTY

Over the years, several political groups have called themselves the Progressive Party. Generally they have stood for liberal social, economic, and political reform.

In 1912 former President Theodore Roosevelt, along with some others, left the Republican Party. They formed the Progressive or Bull Moose Party. The new party supported Roosevelt's unsuccessful 1912 run for the presidency.

In 1924 a group of farm, labor, and religious leaders formed a new Progressive Party. They nominated Senator Robert M. La Follette as their presidential candidate. He received five million votes nationwide but only won a majority of votes in his home state of Wisconsin. The party lasted until the early 1940s, when it merged with the Republican Party.

In 1948 another Progressive Party was formed. Henry A. Wallace was their unsuccessful presidential candidate.

In the 1940s, the Progressive Party supported Henry A. Wallace *(right)* for president. Here, he campaigns with his vice presidential candidate, Glen Taylor.

THE BULL MOOSE PARTY

The Bull Moose or Progressive Party of 1912 was started by former President Theodore Roosevelt. He organized it for a specific purpose. Roosevelt needed a party to support his 1912 run for president.

Theodore Roosevelt had already been president. He served from 1901 to 1909. At that time, he was a Republican. Roosevelt wanted to run for the office again in 1912. But that year, he did not get the Republican Party's nomination, so Roosevelt and his supporters left the party. They started a new party, called the Progressive Party. Its nickname, however, was the Bull Moose Party. The Bull Moose Party's 1912 platform called for many reforms, including programs to preserve the environment. The party also supported women's suffrage—giving women the right to vote.

Roosevelt tried hard to win the presidency. He spent many hours campaigning. Yet he lost the election. The Democratic candidate, Woodrow Wilson, became president instead. Nevertheless, Roosevelt received more votes than the Republican candidate, William Howard Taft.

By 1916 the Bull Moose Party was no longer necessary. Theodore Roosevelt returned to the Republican Party. So did many of his followers. The Bull Moose Party soon fell apart.

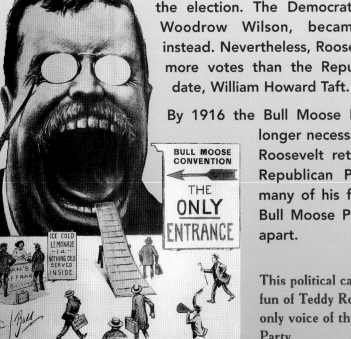

This political cartoon makes fun of Teddy Roosevelt as the only voice of the Bull Moose Party.

H. Ross Perot founded the
Reform Party in 1995.

Wallace was against the "get tough" policy of the United States toward the Soviet Union after World War II.

THE REFORM PARTY

Some third parties have begun more recently. Among these is the Reform Party. Its roots go back to a television talk show. In 1992 the *Larry King Show* featured an unusual guest—billionaire Texas businessman H. Ross Perot. Perot made an announcement that stirred the nation. He said he would run for president on one condition. His supporters would have to get his name on the ballot in every state.

All serious presidential candidates need to be on the ballot. But getting on the ballot is not easy. First, lots of voters must sign petitions. These are lists of people who want a candidate's name placed on the ballot. They show that a large group of people want a person to run for office.

Perot supporters went to work. They began gathering signatures. Perot's name was put on every ballot in the United States. Nevertheless, Perot lost the 1992 presidential election. He did win 20 percent of the vote, however.

LEARN THE LINGO

Perot created political infomercials. Infomercials are half-hour television ads. Perot used them to sell his views to voters during his presidential campaign. He was later named "adman of the year" for his creative infomercials.

WHAT LIBERTARIANS BELIEVE

The Libertarian Party believes that government is the main threat to individual liberties. Libertarians support the repeal (end) of most laws that limit freedom of personal behavior. They also think that private firms should provide many government services. They are against U.S. participation in the United Nations, an international organization dedicated to world peace. The Libertarian Party was founded in 1971.

Perot's supporters refused to give up. They knew that they needed their own political party. In September 1995, Perot and his supporters started the Reform Party.

The idea behind the Reform Party was clear. Its candidates would reform, or change, our nation's government. Reform Party members wanted less government spending. They wanted a balanced budget so the government couldn't spend more money than it had. The party also wanted to simplify the tax code, the system that determines how we are taxed.

In addition, the Reform Party wanted stricter limits on the money political candidates receive. Big companies would not be able to give large amounts of money to candidates. That way the companies would not expect special favors from elected officials.

H. Ross Perot was the Reform Party's 1996 presidential candidate. Once again, he lost the election. But the new party continued.

Jesse Ventura ran for governor of Minnesota in 1998 as a Reform Party candidate. He was certainly a different

DIG DEEPER How can you start a political party? That depends on the state you live in. In some states, you file a form. In others you gather thousands of signatures on petitions. In some states, you form a corporation. In still others, you just pay a filing fee.

Reform Party candidate Jesse Ventura won the race for governor of Minnesota in 1998. He ran against candidates from both the Democratic and Republican Parties.

type of candidate. Often politicians are lawyers or business-people, but Ventura was a wrestler. There had never been a professional wrestler elected governor. Yet Jesse Ventura won the election and became Minnesota's governor.

THE GREEN PARTY

The Green Party is another third party. What do Greens stand for? The party's name gives you a hint. Among other things, Greens are concerned with the environment. They highly value clean air and water. Greens would also like to see more forest and parkland protected. Greens also promote equal rights for everyone.

In the United States, the Green Party started off on a state level during the 1980s. It did not have enough supporters to become a national political party. The Greens wanted to organize throughout the country, however.

After the 1996 elections, the state groups united. They formed the Association of State Green Parties. This group became the Green Party of the United States. It became fairly well known in 2000. That year its presidential candidate was a famous lawyer named Ralph Nader. Nader had long fought for social causes related to public health and safety. He was not afraid to speak out.

Did You KNOW? The Green Party does not only exist in the United States. There are Green Parties in many countries, including Australia, Germany, Finland, Spain, France, New Zealand, and Sweden.

Ralph Nader did not win the election. Yet his candidacy was important. In 2000 fifty-eight Green Party candidates were elected to office.

Ralph Nader, the 2000 Green Party candidate for president, won nearly 3 percent of the vote. This is a lot for a third-party candidate.

New York governor George Pataki campaigns in New York City in 2002. Members of our country's two main political parties, such as Republican Pataki, may find more competition in the future as more and more third-party candidates run for office.

POLITICAL PARTIES IN THE FUTURE

Will a third party in the United States ever become extremely popular? Could one of them rival the two major parties? Might a third party ever replace the Republicans or Democrats?

Third parties continue to challenge old views. They allow different voices to be heard. Political parties in the United States offer voters many choices. That helps our democracy thrive.

GLOSSARY

candidate: a person running for office

delegates: people who represent other people at meetings and conventions

democracy: a form of government in which the people choose their leaders

inauguration: the ceremony at which an elected official is sworn in

majority party: the political party in power

minority party: the political party out of power

nominate: to choose someone to run for office

oppose: to be against something

party platform: a statement of a political party's stands on important issues

reform: to change something for the better

regulations: rules

streamline: to make something simpler or more efficient

surplus: an amount that is more than is needed

tariff: a tax on goods coming into the United States

third party: a major political party that exists alongside two main parties, in a country where the two main parties are usually the most powerful

SOURCE NOTES

For quoted material: p. 15, Baker, Daniel B. ed., Political Quotations (Detroit: Gale Research, 1990), 148; p. 16, Democratic National Committee website, <http://www.democrats.org/about/history.html >; p. 21, Republican National Committee website, <http://www.rnc.org/gopinfo/history>; p. 23, Abraham Lincoln, Speech at the Republican State Convention, Springfield, Illinois, June 16, 1858; p. 35, National Federation of Republican Women, <http://www.nfrw.org/republicans/principles.htm>; p. 42, the Socialist Party U.S.A. website, <http://sp-usa.org>.

BIBLIOGRAPHY

Baer, Kenneth. *Reinventing Democrats*. Lawrence, KS: University Press of Kansas, 2000.

Batchelor, John Calvin. *"Ain't You Glad You Joined the Republicans?"* New York: Henry Holt and Company, 1996.

Brown, Peter. *Minority Party; Why Democrats Face Defeat in 1992 and Beyond*. Washington, D.C.: Regnery Gateway, 1991.

Eldersveld, Samuel J. *Political Parties in American Society*. New York: Palgrave, 1999.

Gerring, John. *Party Ideologies in America*. New York: Cambridge University Press, 2001.

Gillespie, J. David. *Politics at the Periphery: Third Parties in Two-Party America*. Columbia, SC: University of South Carolina Press, 1993.

Lentz, Jacob. *Electing Jesse Ventura: A Third Party Success Story*. Boulder, CO: Lynne Rienner Publishers, 2001.

Nader, Ralph. *Crashing the Party: How to Tell the Truth and Still Run for President*. New York: St. Martin's Press, 2002.

Nichols, Roy F. *The Invention of the American Political Parties*. New York: Macmillan, 1967.

Perot, H. Ross. *United We Stand: How We Can Take Back Our Country*. New York: Hyperion, 1992.

Posner, Gerald. *Citizen Perot: His Life and Times*. New York: Random House, 1996.

Resenbrink, John, and Ralph Nader. *Against All Odds: The Full Transformation of American Politics*. Raymond, ME: Leopold Press, 1999.

Rutland, Robert Allen. *The Republicans: From Lincoln to Bush*. Columbia, MO: University of Missouri Press, 1996.

Rutland, Robert Allen, and Jimmy Carter. *The Democrats: From Jefferson to Clinton*. Columbia, MO: University of Missouri Press, 1995.

WEBSITES

Democratic National Committee
<http://www.democrats.org>

Green Party of the United States
<http://www.greenpartyus.org>

Reform Party Official Website
<http://www.reformparty.org>

Republican National Committee
<http://www.rnc.org>

The White House
<http://www.whitehouse.gov>

FURTHER READING

Collier, Christopher, and James Lincoln Collier. *Andrew Jackson's America, 1824–1850*. Tarrytown, NY: Benchmark Books, 1999.

Fish Durost, Bruce, and Becky Fish Durost. *The History of the Democratic Party*. Broomall, PA: Chelsea House, 1999.

Harvey, Miles. *Presidential Elections*. Danbury, CT: Children's Press, 1996.

Henry, Christopher E. *Presidential Conventions*. Danbury, CT: Franklin Watts, 1996.

Jones, Veda Boyd. *Government and Politics*. Broomall, PA: Chelsea House, 1999.

Kowalski, Kathiann. *Campaign Politics: What's Fair? What's Foul?* Minneapolis: Lerner Publications Company, 2001.

Kronenwetter, Michael. *Political Parties of the United States*. Berkeley Heights, NJ: Enslow, 1996.

Levy, Debbie. *Lyndon B. Johnson*. Minneapolis: Lerner Publications Company, 2003.

Lindop, Edmund. *Political Parties.* Brookfield, CT: Twenty-First Century Books, 1996.

Lutz, Norma Jean. *The History of the Republican Party.* Broomall, PA: Chelsea House, 2000.

Morin, Isobel V. *Politics, American Style: Political Parties in American History.* Brookfield, CT: Twenty-First Century, 1999.

Roberts, Jeremy. *Abraham Lincoln.* Minneapolis: Lerner Publications Company, 2004.

———. *Franklin D. Roosevelt.* Minneapolis: Lerner Publications Company, 2003.

Sullivan, George. *Choosing the Candidates.* Englewood Cliffs, NJ: Silver Burdett, 1991.

WEBSITES

The History of Political Parties
<www.americanhistory.about.com/cs/politicalparties/>
This site offers a look at our nation's political parties—both past and present.

Life at the Conventions—1948–1996
<www.lifemag.com/life/conventions/>
Enjoy this web gallery of great photos. They capture all the excitement of political party national conventions over a half-century.

The PBS Kids Democracy Project
<www.pbs.org/democracy/kids/educators>
What is government? What role does it play in our lives? Why do we need government? The answers are at this website.

INDEX

About the Author

Award-winning children's book author Elaine Landau worked as a newspaper reporter, a children's book editor, and a youth services librarian before becoming a full-time writer. She has written more than two hundred nonfiction books for young readers. Ms. Landau has a bachelor's degree in English and journalism from New York University and a master's degree in library and information science from Pratt Institute. She lives in Miami, Florida, with her husband, Norman, and her son, Michael. You can visit Elaine Landau at her website <www.elainelandau.com>.

Photo Acknowledgments

Photographs in this book appear with the permission of: © Frances M. Roberts, pp. 4, 11, 49; © Richard B. Levine, pp. 5, 7, 8, 35, 45, 48; © Philip Gould/CORBIS, p. 6; Southdale-Hennepin County Library, p. 9; © AFP/CORBIS, pp. 10, 40; © North Wind Picture Archive, p. 13; National Gallery of Art, Washington, D.C., p. 14; American Philosophical Society, p. 16; Library of Congress, pp. 18, 19, 20, 22, 25 (right), 28, 32, 41; Schomburg Center for Research in Black Culture, p. 21; Dictionary of American Portraits, p. 24; National Archives, p. 25 (left); © Jim West, p. 27; Franklin D. Roosevelt Library, pp. 29, 30; © Bettmann/CORBIS, pp. 31, 34; Jim Simondet/IPS, p. 36; © Underwood & Underwood/CORBIS, p. 42; Brown Brothers, pp. 43, 44; Star Tribune, p. 47.